LEXINGTON PUBLIC LIBRARY

WE CELEBRATE HALLOWEEN IN FALL

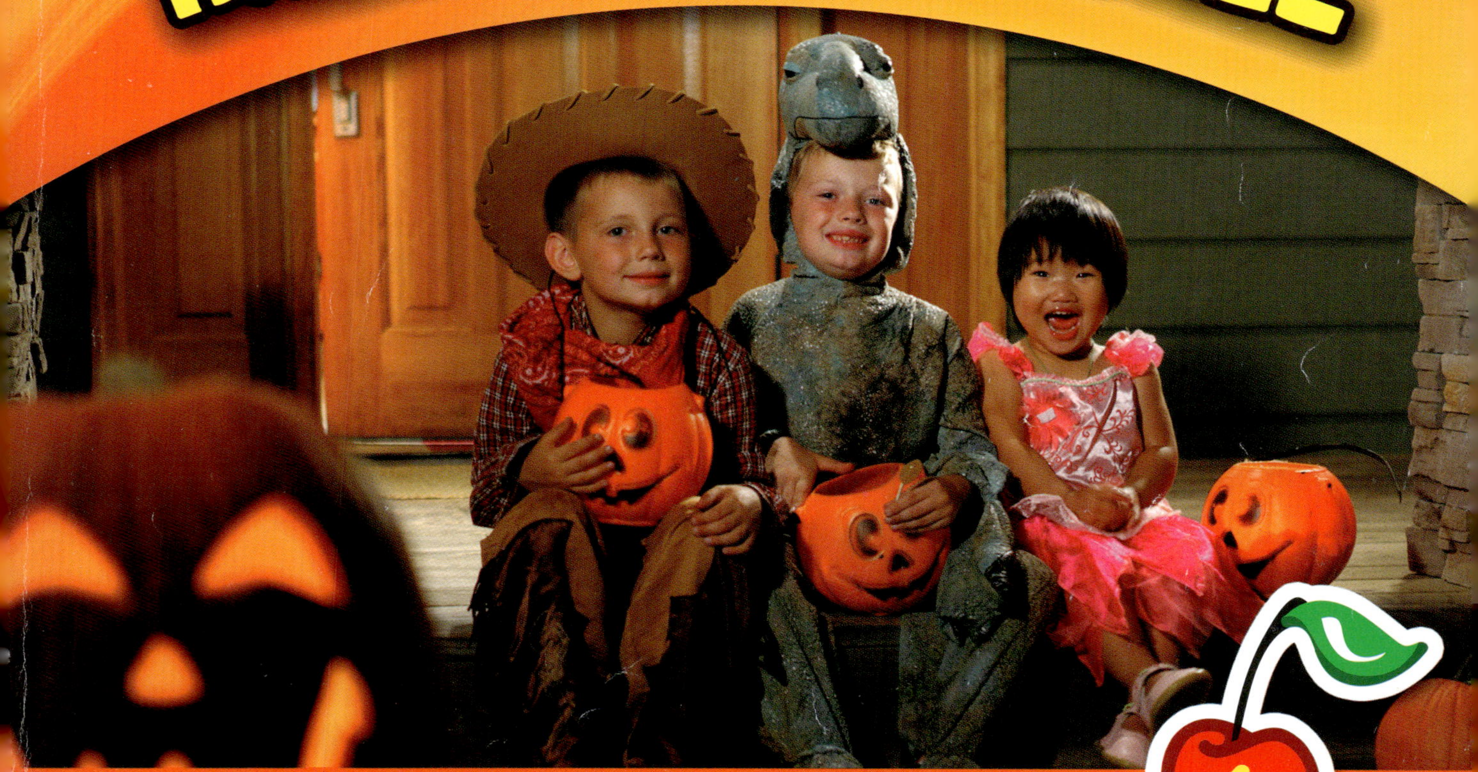

by Rebecca Felix

Cherry Lake Publishing • Ann Arbor, Michigan

1

Published in the United States of America
by Cherry Lake Publishing
Ann Arbor, Michigan
www.cherrylakepublishing.com

Consultant: Marla Conn, Read-Ability

Photo Credits: Morgan Lane Studios/iStockphoto, cover, 1; Losevsky Photo and Video/Shutterstock Images, 4; PhotoFixPics/Shutterstock Images, 6; Blend Images/Shutterstock Images, 8; Johanna Goodyear/Shutterstock Images, 10; Brazhnykov Andriy/Shutterstock Images, 12; Agnieszka Kirinicjanow/iStockphoto, 14; Kali Nine LLC/iStockphoto, 16; Catherine Yeulet/iStockphoto, 18; Monkey Business Images/Shutterstock Images, 20

Copyright ©2013 by Cherry Lake Publishing
All rights reserved. No part of this book may be reproduced or utilized in any form or by any means without written permission from the publisher.

Library of Congress Cataloging-in-Publication Data
Felix, Rebecca, 1984-
  We celebrate Halloween in fall / Rebecca Felix.
      p. cm. -- (Let's look at fall)
  Includes index.
  ISBN 978-1-61080-903-0 (hardback : alk. paper) -- ISBN 978-1-61080-928-3 (paperback : alk. paper) -- ISBN 978-1-61080-953-5 (ebook) -- ISBN 978-1-61080-978-8 (hosted ebook)
 1. Halloween--Juvenile literature. I. Title.

GT4965.F45 2013
394.2646--dc23

2012030455

Cherry Lake Publishing would like to acknowledge the work of The Partnership for 21st Century Skills. Please visit www.21stcenturyskills.org for more information.

Printed in the United States of America
Corporate Graphics Inc.
January 2013
CLFA10

TABLE OF CONTENTS

- **5**   **Fall is Here**
- **9**   **Fun**
- **13**   **Dress-Up**
- **17**   **Treats**
- **21**   **November**

- 22   Find Out More
- 22   Glossary
- 23   Home and School Connection
- 23   What Do You See?
- 24   Index
- 24   About the Author

Fall is Here

Fall is a season. Weather gets colder. A fun holiday is coming!

What Do You See?

How many ghosts do you see?

Halloween is on October 31.
It is a spooky holiday!

Fun

People **celebrate** in many ways. Eve **carves** a pumpkin.

Some people celebrate scary things. They go to haunted houses.

Dress-Up

Many people make or buy **costumes**. Jan buys a fun dress and hat.

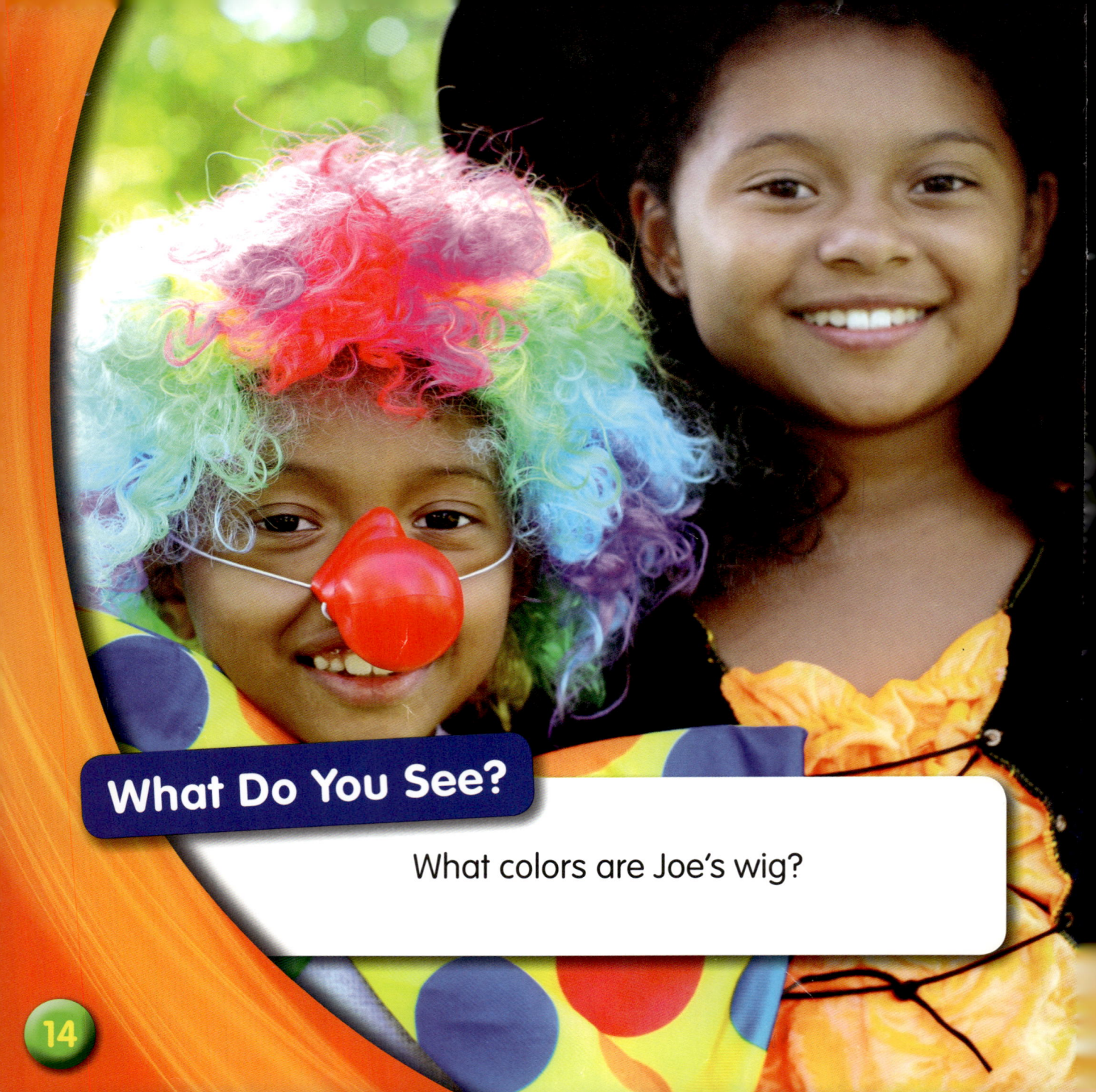

What Do You See?

What colors are Joe's wig?

People dress up as many things! Joe is a clown. Meg is a witch.

What Do You See?

What costumes do you see?

Treats

Kids **trick-or-treat**. Zach and his friend go to houses and ask for candy.

Sam's class has a party.
They eat fun treats.

November

After Halloween, November starts. What holiday is next?

Find Out More

BOOK
Marsh, Laura. *National Geographic Readers: Halloween*. Washington, DC: National Geographic Children's Books, 2012.

WEB SITE
Happy Halloween—PBS Kids
pbskids.org/halloween/
Find fun Halloween stories, activities, and games.

Glossary

carves (KAHRVS) forms or makes pieces by cutting

celebrate (SEL-uh-brate) to enjoy an event or holiday with others

costumes (KAHS-tooms) outfits people wear to look like something or someone else

trick-or-treat (TRIK-or-treet) to go to houses and ask for candy on Halloween

Home and School Connection

Use this list of words from the book to help your child become a better reader. Word games and writing activities can help beginning readers reinforce literacy skills.

candy	dress-up	holiday	scary
carves	eat	houses	season
celebrate	fall	kids	spooky
class	fun	November	treats
clown	ghosts	October	trick-or-treat
colder	Halloween	party	weather
costumes	hat	people	witch
dress	haunted	pumpkin	

What Do You See?

What Do You See? is a feature paired with select photos in this book. It encourages young readers to interact with visual images in order to build the ability to integrate content in various media formats.

You can help your child further evaluate photos in this book with additional activities. Look at the images in the book without the What Do You See? feature. Ask your child to describe one detail in each image, such as a costume, treat, or activity.

Index

carves, 9
costumes, 13, 14, 15, 16

haunted houses, 11

November, 21

October, 7

pumpkin, 9

treats, 17, 19
trick-or-treat, 17

weather, 5

About the Author

Rebecca Felix is an editor and writer from Minnesota. She dresses up for Halloween every year. One year she dressed as a fortune teller!